SEVEN

SEVEN

For information, contact 3: A Taos Press, P.O. Box 370627, Denver, CO 80237

Published by 3: A Taos Press

ISBN: 978-0-9847925-1-1

First U.S. edition 2013

Book Design and Cover: Andrew Mendez, Los Angeles, CA
Press Logo Design: William Watson, Castro Watson Design, New York, NY
Cover Photograph: Published by permission of Brooke Shaden, Los Angeles, CA
Author Photograph: Paul Gutierrez, Arvada, CO

Printed in the United States of America by Cottrell Printing Company

www.3taospress.com

SEVEN

poems

Sheryl Luna

3: A Taos Press

Books by Sheryl Luna

Pity the Drowned Horses

Winner of the Andres Montoya Poetry Prize

Acknowledgments

Grateful acknowledgment is made to editors of the following publications and websites in which some of these poems originally appeared, sometimes in earlier forms: *Huizache,* "Universal Kiss" and "La Chingada"; *Ensemble Jourine,* "Kitchen Of Grief"; *Bordersenses,* "Forty Days", "Brandy Down", and "Our Throats Like Fire"; *Valparaiso Poetry Review,* "Elegy For Narcissus"; *Bridges: A Feminist Journal,* "The Healing Poem"; *Standards: International Cultural Studies,* "Lubbock, Texas 1981"; *American Literary Review,* "Mortar"; *Wisconsin Review,* "Alluvial Heartache"; *Margie,* "Coming Home" and "Born In The Southwest"; *Numéro Cinq,* "Equus", "Cabeza De Vaca's Horse", "Writing The Next Poem", and "Small Defiant Gods"; *Many Mountains Moving,* "This Is The Wintry Season" and "The Flowers Coming Soon"; *Acentos Review,* "This Is The Way We Come To Light"; *Copper Nickel,* "On Innocence"; *Feminist Studies,* "Chico's Tacos"; and *Women's Studies Quarterly,* "Beginning And Ending".

I would like to thank the following residencies, individuals and organizations which provided much needed time and space to work on these poems: Sandra Cisneros for the Alfredo Cisneros del Moral Foundation Award, Dagoberto Gilb and Christine Granados for the nominations, the Ragdale Foundation, the Anderson Center, the Corporation of Yaddo, the Guild Literary Complex and Letras Latinas at the University of Notre Dame. I also am forever thankful for the friends and fellow poets and writers who helped through encouragement and a careful eye. It is a pleasure to thank Wendy Abbiati, Eduardo Corral, Fran Ford, Christine Granados, Bryan Roth, Lew Forrester, Carmen Seda, Paul Gutierrez and Gwen Sonstroem. Also, a big thanks to Amy Moore and the folks at JCMH. It is a real pleasure to thank the wonderful editors at 3: A Taos Press, Andrea Watson and Madelyn Garner, for their patience, skilled editing and kindness. I am grateful for the support of the acquisitions editor, Veronica Golos. I'd like to thank my former teachers for their wisdom and guidance with the writing: Leslie Ullman, Bruce Bond, Benjamin Saenz, Daniel Chacon and Lex Williford. Much gratitude goes out to the CantoMundo fellows, faculty and founding members. Finally, I have great appreciation for my family's steadfast support.

Contents

Envidia, orgullo/benevolencia, amabilidad, humilidad

Gula, glotonería/codicia, ambicíon, avidez

Codicia, ambicíon, avidez/benevolencia, caridad

Envidia/benevolencia, amabilidad

In memory of Sharon Niles and Janet Gates

SEVEN

Seven

Martes a party, Lunes, a tide pulling you dark. Miércoles,
a miracle. Viernes sounding old. Viejita, her forlorn
wisdom wanders, like a ghost. Thursday full of thirst.
Friday a pit-roast. Sábado sexy.
Sombrero a Sabbath. Domingo as host.

How many times should we forgive? Prime #. Seven
times Seven. Jacob's seven-year service to Rachel
turned to love. Once seven spheres in space coiled
heaven. Mercury is a hot-burn close to the fire light
that's us. Venus holds a lusty lease on the sun.
Who can forgive trespasses slick, feigned love?

Mars a red desert and Saturn ringed
in dust. Uranus, planet of philanthropy,
prone to distrust. Moses bewildered and naked pale
in the wilderness heard the Alpha, the Omega burn.
His synapses ablaze. In the beginning was the word,
the universe a wordless hum of dust and light.

Cold emptiness. Stars like lamps, named for mythical
heroes. Orion with his war shield seen
for centuries clutching a sword. We learned to kill
early and kill well. Wisdom's house built on seven
columns, and there are seven deadly sins and seven
virtues. It is said God formed everything in seven
days, and our days and nights but a cast stone, sparked.

✲ ✲ ✲

Ira, furor, rabia/paciencia
Anger, fury, rage/patience

"Patience is passion tamed."

— Lyman Abbot

"I was angry with my friend: I told my wrath, my wrath did end.
I was angry with my foe: I told it not, my wrath did grow."

— William Blake

Equus

If you try to ruin me, saddle me with man-made
doubt, I'll gallop past large pines.

Aspen will bleed, fall as I run forgotten trails, seeking
a sunlit path.

My sway back will sweat slick. Arctic and blazing,
I'll grow wild,
rear up and kick.

If you try to break me, remember, I'm a maverick on a mad run.

Corral me?
Herd me?

A lasso burns my thick neck.

Use me like property?
Cage me and blame me?

I'm hard-hoofed, snickered trouble.

Just when you think you've won,
I'll buck.

The Breaking

We break and rise as the ocean, moon and stars.
Silence follows.

Were we meant to unhinge?

Low beat of morning.
We crack like children's bones;
mending is possible. The letting-go like dawn.

The piano keys strike
in time to the light shimmered pines.
We are plural and singular sadness,
broken in the high desert when snow refuses to melt.
Streetlights lull against the darkness.

Bats shrieking, bellow of strange heaven;
bats of bendable bones hang
in their upside-down thrones. Caverns light
with their darkness. Stalactites shimmer
with man-made lights.

Snaps of the mind: circling, turmoil in nets, flight.
A burst of shade flaps madly by the thousands.
This is the old dusk, the dark awakening.

But we break as glorious as whales breach seas,
as if we too must suddenly
and spectacularly breathe.

Atonement

Before you died, you said the planets could sing.

I am still waiting.

Rage is a frozen ending to unfulfilled dreams.
The sea sweeps us past the gulf to the bayou.

We are two Mardi Gras beaded tricksters dancing
towards the dark, our fathers predators.

I will forever make amends for my rages.

Will you come to my dreams?

There is nothing left. You are gone.
There are a billion stars we've stumbled on

and time is a dream where we forgot how to see.
I'm counting small stars as the eye
of the galaxy watches us.

The confessional always too dark
and the priest's rough hands ice on my knees.
He shakes my arms, says I've put nails through Jesus' hands.

Years later on a cold Louisiana night, we walk
like two dogs about the blackest lake
searching for light.

La Chingada

She collected branches for her burning, limping
        on a once broken ankle. Cortez advised we cook
in the stillness before sunrise. The crowd
        amicable. He said, "Look to the stars."
A New Mexico chill drifted through the wind.

        Vultures carried off the dead. Cortez built himself a cragged nest tangled
in bare branches. I ask no questions of the dead. My throat
        is a ravenous caw, and here she comes again resurrected

in the labyrinth of story. La Malinche whispers in my ear,
        "Cortez only lives in your head."

                ❁ ❁ ❁

Mother, why do you lie?
        You said, "Cortez is kind."
Cortez and his black cigars and lies,
        his Zippo and flame to cigarette.

Click. Winter has come to the desert.
        Nine below. Icy snow and the roads unclean.
A memory of groaning sandstorms cleanses.

Malinche walks in ink-black evening, calls me friend.
        Her lips magenta with wine. What is pretending,
but believing our own lies?

Cortez and his black boots, sword polished, sharpened,
        stained. Later, Malinche with the Zippo in her hands,
nails painted black. He looks disinterested or pleased

with himself. God-Man. Altar of what's not willingly
        sacrificed. You worshipped him, Mother,
and this has been the crutch of my bad temper.

You kissed his dark feet, and you will never
        allow yourself to hear silence.
You said, "Speak only the language of silence."

        Your throat a river of smoke.

Yes, Malinche, you conflate
        with a million packs of cigarettes
and leave only ash. All night we burned.

        We were meant for it, we know. Doña Marina,
why must we drink this cup?
        You led us once through jungle,
dark mediator, liaison to priests hung like animals.

        Every sacrifice screamed from their lips.
The villagers demand strength,
        and we are dark with it. It is time to sing.

Must we continue to rob ourselves?
        Cortez was a thief, Mother, nothing more.
This is the time for atonement. We can rip
        all the flowers, the dirt beneath our nails black.

I Was Once The Dusty Ramble Of Desert Weeds

Sandstorms, the arroyo filled with sharp rocks
and scorpions. I was once dark as a night with no stars—
the cloudiness of storm and hardship.

It came as a dream, the hands of laborers,
the vision of hopeful children, after the breaking.
And she, a feminist, said to the world, we must not show
such brokenness. I was the rape she anthologized,
the bruises she anesthetized.

I was the dream and the nightmare.
I saw their healing palms on the river of Lethe,
where they helped me remember myself.
All the scholars left the scene.

I was no bookish thing, too broken for talking to.

One wrote beautifully of wings, another marched
with a flag streaming like my madness.

Who was it that taught me to listen?
She is dead and buried, alive in the sunlight
beside a stream, where damselflies
of every color sit with a stillness I cannot forget.

I was once the moon glow on a dying lake,
the lone bare tree there cragged and emptying.
Today, I find we all break and then, like rainbows
 or desert wildflowers, bloom in the listening,
in the forgiving, and every abstraction takes its toll.

I am the breakthrough river poem, the wildfire,
the thoroughbred.

The Memory

When I was a child I dreamed every Bible white.
Jesus' broth-filled eyes condemned. Men were dangerous.

Now I worship trees, the breath of coming spring,
see myself float in clear waters. The anger gone.

I awaken to the sound of birds, the breath of morning,
evergreen branches covered in a blanket of white.

Some things don't belong in poems,
unbeautiful and brutal—swollen blue-black
bruises, a circular patch of broken
blood-vessels on a child.

My father shape-shifted to an animal,
but the brutal act pressed down
past my awareness, like breath and death.

The sun streams, and I survive in a dream.
Awake I lash out, rage,
unsure why. The clouds a tumult of fire,
images of my dead father's face swelter in clouds.

Resurrections once helped me
forget: Jesus suffering, angels sailing dream-like and singing.
The memory came a hurricane, tsunami,
wreckage of sky and lakes.

I see finally, the veil lifting. Wedding
suddenly to awareness,
the rain bounces on asphalt,
the hail of it coming down to cleanse.

Afterwards, I become light along treetops,
the steamy green of giant firs.

A Contentious Woman Speaks

My shame is a cloak,
and it knows an old bridge's
rickety pain. The flat rat did not run past the season.
The small fox contains a melody.
The braggart's packaged himself
in a box with a red bow.

I am slow in morning light, silent
in dawn's coming breath. Robins larger than I've seen,
even bats flutter morning. I refuse to paint clear waters,

a herd of clouds following emptied space
and solitude. I envied his ways
three decades and forty-seven days, envied
his clucking tongue, his relentless mantra
pecking away,

his strange flock following after,
clucking the same cluck. The goats gnaw
weeds through the white fence, one fat albino
rat emerges amidst darkness from the brush.

He buys mansions for himself and will build you a shack.
Multitudes follow hoping to touch his red cape.
They have built him a shrine and melt fool's gold
for his cane. He carries it to abuse what is beautiful,

carries it to beat a poet to death saying, "I am a good man."
He is bald and tells tales where he is always the hero,
but he saves only liars.

I live on the corner of the rooftop.
The liar insists on the value of lying.
He puts me out
on the edge of the house. The cut worm
cannot forgive the plow. It is winter in Colorado,
and the streetlamps shed
the afterglow of talk.

✦ ✦ ✦

Lujuria, ansia/castidad
Lust, longing/chastity

"Chastity does not mean abstention from sexual wrong;
it means something flaming, like Joan of Arc."

— Gilbert Keith Chesterton

"Whether we fall by ambition, blood or dust, like
diamonds we are cut with our own dust."

— John Weber

The Photograph

A black glove fastens
my mouth shut.

I stir to awareness;
       I've slept three decades,

gaze into a stranger's face, feel
       a breeze against bare breasts.

Confusion later at my sore body,
       "What did they do to me?"

But the question, the scene
       the jerking violence, my legs

high above my head, forgotten.

I later find myself in a black brazier
that isn't mine, how it got there,
takes a moment, a lifetime.
Fog in my mind lifts.

His smile, slanted, pleased
       with a charade of power—

I rise, remove the bra, throw it from a shadow
       in the hall, forget

       for decades the camera shot, me
asleep in a drug-haze.

"No one will believe you," he says.
             But I have already forgotten.

And they tell me there are no victims.

Only in the condescension of the oldest lie

can a woman rise, find her own power.

The Hunger Of Forgetting

We grew so large the roof jarred to the left.
        The neighbors pretended not to hear the groan.

Bricks cracked and the void
        opened itself up
like a bottle of Jim Beam.

        But nobody drank.

We were heavy for sustenance,
        and prayer was an afterthought.

Father-figure said to me nightly,
        "Keep your elbow off the damn table."

Now when I'm at a restaurant I watch everyone's elbows rest,
        the clamor of talk rambunctious.

I am always conscious,
        ate eighteen years without touching the table.

Windows are lit with the only sun we know.

        A picture of Jesus followed me about the house,
floating eyes always on my body,
        my back, legs, arms, my breasts. Colors
like blood; the pitch of shame lined my throat.

        Jesus must have known of the sin.
Silence hovered and stung.

I grew obsessed with forgetting,
began to breathe careful breaths
        calming myself, overwhelmed,

I lived alone in large empty spaces,
        grew so large the entire neighborhood
heard my obnoxious snores;
        the chomp of my gum
thundered in the late afternoon.
        Leaving Texas, unconsciously

the Continental Divide, the Sierras,

        split—
                uncertain of the new
        name

        conjured, brewed and broken,
I continued to grow—smothered friends,
        wrote long songs and mastered the art
        of lying.

Mumbling hearts rang in my red ears.
        When my step-father died,
stuck with the sharp pen
        of memory, I cracked open.

A father—
        sodomy
        two of his friends
        forgotten—

My body floating outside itself,
        father nude but for white socks.

The memory came with two questions,
        "Who is this man?" "What happened?"

I now ask my lover to remove his socks.
        My voice hot air and solitude.

In the end I learned to eat with my elbows
        and hands on the table to the relief of all.

I'm growing smaller and smaller. Soon
        there will be room for you too.

Brandy Down

I worshipped his sinewy leg,
savored his chest that still swims in my mind.
He spoke some wisdom at twenty. A manly-prince,
meaty wish, a runner in spiked shoes.
Sockless and fast on the track,
body glinting and light. We were running and rumba
out on endless plains. We were sagebrush on fire.

We listened to Bob Dylan, and the snow
fell like wildfire. The nights were still.
Sunflowers behind the barn, dinosaur eggs
petrified in the valley. We were sure of it:
everything dawn. His blue singlet
dashing in the breeze. Record mile time,
marijuana, amaretto.

Lubbock had one hill. We ran it like desire.
Over and over again. We ran it in mud and mire. I
grew dark and my arms and thighs
knew only longing. Roberto and Camille shameless
in the chapel. The Baptist preacher screamed
they were destined for hell.

Our Throats Like Fire

When I die,
I will imagine his brown eyes. I will die
again and again at 19, shouting out, *"My life! My life!"*

"Am I sexy?" he asked dark faced beneath the sky's
moonlit pond. He was sexy like a poem.

But I did not answer. He was sex-charged brandy
and disaster. A cop ruined our fun, flashlight
falling on us.

He was a luminous lighthouse in my chest.
I live him again and again, though I've been long dead.
I remember the certain living fire.

Find me at the cragged cliff, ablaze and filled
with old religion, my hymn unrighteous, the boats traveling
darkness like an old language.

Kitchen Of Grief

Every broken thing stored
and restored. The cabinets are locked.

My mind lets loose as pool balls break.
Smoke unravels to nothingness.

I am hot
and hungry, weighing time
with emptiness.

The oven's crackled for days.
If I speak
no one listens.

Accustomed to solitude
I whisper,

cook meaninglessness,
bake it dark
above blue flames.

The last bulb projects
a pale yellow flower
on the ceiling.

When will fire arrive? The sun?

Lead me into temptation.
My blood is mercurial.

My kitchen prepares nothing
for this world. They say hell
is an endless burn.

Such thirst.

Such fire.

On Innocence

He wants a poem about a woman's body
trim and dark, eyes dank as dreamless sleep
water-wet for sex. He speaks loneliness,
wears no shoes and sinks in high tide.

The sky fills fluttering with gulls.
He forgets what it is to sing.

His thighs long and thin, eyes seeking fires and storms.

It's all he knows, tumult and double-full.

❂ ❂ ❂

She is a pale shell that keeps the secret music
deep beneath her skirt. Shy like a house finch
amid summer's tangled branches and leaves.

Light on the deck, she sees what's lost.

Some days she refuses to speak.
Her teal eyes watch tide subside.

He's a night-brawler,
Harley high, roaring down a highway lit
with streetlamps. Snow falls unhurried.

He's known his father-preacher's fist,
known his mother's last kiss.

Rabble-rouser, doused in cocktail blues,
dancing in rebel jeans, gun tucked close,
six-pack torso. He's headed to trouble,
born to it like a left hook.

❀ ❀ ❀

She wears a denim skirt,
hands pat it down in the breeze;
she takes ballroom dance classes.

She knew how to rock,
smoked marijuana in the summer of 1972.

"Rough sex all night long," she says. Now,
she grooms a white stallion before rain comes,
drowning all other sounds.

The desert glows like fire.

❀ ❀ ❀

Afraid to die,
we seek a flash, falling star,

seek to know ourselves,
to forget ourselves.

And who am I or you that we long
for something we can never have back?

Beginning And Ending

We were new worlds, hemp and happiness.
We were clothed in ritual and geometry.
We started again and again, shone star-like
bold and blue.
Explosive, his eyes made me wild.

We were bipolar bliss,
euphoria in a dream of we.
We were Buddha consejos restored,
a tiny bit of technology beeping.

And what's it all for?

This strange waking, this surreal dreaming?
We are breath, robins and morning coming
again and again. The poem a half- hearted effort
toward wholeness. Once you said I was an ocean,

the real me, waves and waves, nothing but rising
and fading emotion. We were bigger
than waves for a while: talking, breathing, eating.

I saw starlight in his eyes and every critic
weeps in solitude, for we are a hip-hop dance
about the totem before rain falls. This is the beginning

of wholeness and growth. There is no time
for judgment. Maybe we are learning to live,
on the precipice of our life's end.

Universal Kiss

There were three fates spinning thread,
spinning our lives, saying *clip here*
and fray there. Jonah worried three days
in a whale. The monster yet unnamed.
The father, the son, and spirit—One
and three divisible by only themselves.
Three-fold and evolutionary, he said, "I rise anew."
The sound of thorns and thrashing, thimble
and sewing—all the mending, the folding
too, all this for the harvest threshing.
Our throats ring of it, sing of it. Holy, Holy,
the perfect number. Thunder throws us down.
Thirty pieces of silver and Three betrayed;
we can't have a God that goes un-screwed.
His number thrums in space. And Her temple
torn down only to be rebuilt in words.
She was goddess, lover, a universal kiss.
This is the beginning, she laughed. I am. I am.

Pereza/diligencia
Idleness/diligence

"Expect poison from standing water."

— William Blake

"The expectations of life depend on diligence; the mechanic that would perfect his work must first sharpen his tools."

— Confucius

Crazy Ted Talks To La Virgen De Guadalupe

He lights candles to la Virgen de Guadalupe,
rocks as he sits shoulders sloped, legs crossed.
A black rosary rises and falls against his heart.
The altar candles in his room burn down.

His head is large and his eyes bulge bipolar.
At six feet two he walks the streets,
sweating, big palm clenched
like an oyster shell about a pearl.

He carries a plastic black rosary, each bead
rubbed dull by an obsessive thumb, each prayer
an urgent rendition towards desire.
He says, "I'll have a higher place in heaven

than you." He wants to join a monastery
in Arkansas, walk among monks, heads
bowed and shaven. He chants to angels,
the dead, nobody else can see,

smokes cigarettes beyond
the filter, lives for the ashes, the clichéd
dark night of his soul. Reality eggs him on at times,
but he'll have none of it.

He writes novels about God's corporation
where he's the CEO and sells a zillion t-shirts
of Jesus doing push-ups
to fans in sold out stadiums.

It's all about the marketing, he insists,
even a poem or a God.

This Is The Wintry Season

Overcome with shame, the neighbor feeds
lettuce to the local rabbit.
Boys upstairs smoke crack and the light
in the basement leads them to contend
with an air-conditioner gone awry,
heat swarming their bodies.
I have a quiet place to write.

I suddenly feel like drinking,
like Raymond Carver. I feel like Raymond Carver
minus the spouse, children and purpose.

I go outside in the heat and sit, and begin
to type, hoping something will come,
that business and marketing fiends haven't sapped me.

I am less than bare trees,
remembering the evergreen weighed down with snow.
I am less than taxes paid.
Music comes forth, to the rhythm of cars on the highway.

The moon is absent, the wind is furnace and mirage,
the rabbit nowhere to be found.
How to lose the self, the sudden desire for winning?

Music takes us towards
ourselves and away. Or is it the sun and stars?
Everything outside ourselves,
still and sullen in the moment.

What do I hear?

Traffic and drops of rain in puddles,
the click and patter
of computer keys, the cooling realization
there's nothing to win.

The Flowers Coming Soon

She falls slowly asleep, crumpled
over her legs. A man on the bus asks if she's okay.
This is the way we grow bitter. Poverty-lined face,
garbage bag of clothes. She nods off, hand stretched
protectively into the bag. Another man places

a green towel over his too thin legs, pats it down.
You take a second look; it's not a skirt.
This is the way people go down under
with white cumulous clouds and two gulls
barking into the blue.

Another woman with tattoos down her arms says,
"I have six disorders. I'm on SSI.
I take Serequel, Prozac, lithium," unashamed.
Strange disorders, where one imagines
dead spirits of friends riding on the wings
of damselflies, the dead speaking
our true names.

This is the disorder of society, seething with rage,
gifts of small change. Counting quarters and begging
for bus fare, the poor are shamed into silence.
Branches of these oaks bare against clouds, birds
dart whirling in a pattern, and I think of a falcon,
hooded and perched on my teacher's gloved hand,
bird of prey on a leash.

Vultures at the Denver Zoo with wings
cut with scissors. We are but small miracles, tax debts
washed away by the sun. We study the homeless, some bitter
like the desert wind. We study their mannerisms,
ruffled hair, set in odd ways, leaning left, as if to say,
"I no longer give a shit." We too with mirrors,
diving like cormorants into dark waters.

We are after all fishermen, kings or serfs, but the sky
and waters lend us this time to see, hear and touch
what is underway. Moment to moment, meal to meal.
Scarcity to wealth, blessing to curse. And we study our Buddha,
our Jesus, our fools, our postmodern leanings,
glad the flowers will burst open soon.

El Pescador

Fishermen once threw horses overboard as a sacrifice to Poseidon.

— *after Jane Harrison*

A fly-caster with a hook seeks Colorado trout in sunlight.
        Spotted and dying, they swim upstream
while scientists try to preserve genes.

For millennia they've spawned, fed, bled.

They are drawn into water currents
        by duende's sleek force:
a galaxy of spreading stars,

history, and a muscled salmon dawn.

A hook's silver light snaps the stream.

        Evolutionists say we're born of cerulean ooze,
        with it in the womb.

And what have we sacrificed?
        Any living thing will do—
Man-God, a body flung overboard,
        so we can hook and reel

the brute within.

Smarter Than Everyone Else

Homeless since August he says, "I was raised by Nazis."
He says, "If I lose everything, that will be the end,"
and though he laughs, his vagrancy

mocks him. Pride in every detail, handwriting
old-school architectural, books in plastic bags
snug in a spotless backpack.

Bob Marley's "Three Little Birds" playing
in the background. All is not well, and we hold to what we know
like parasites. He wears the same green shirt day to day,

stays up all night in cafés, sleeps where he can during the day.
Couch surfing, he avoids shelters, afraid his laptop
will disappear. He needs it to avoid reality.

"Don't worry," a foolish headline for the masses?
And I hear something in the blue sky, a melody
of geese and grackles tuned to house finches in spring.

"Don't worry," he says to me, "life is shit."
About to lose every possession, and about to seek a gun,
he's pissed about living under the loam of a hefty intellect,
the kind that makes one feel smarter than everyone else.

❀ ❀ ❀

Envidia, orgullo/benevolencia, amabilidad, humilidad

Envy, pride/benevolence, kindness, humility

"Envy is the ulcer of the soul."

— Socrates

"Be kind to unkind people—they need it the most."

— Ashleigh Brilliant

Bucephalus

— sculpture by Al Wadzinski, 1998, found object art

Hubcaps, pipes, engine parts, hooves of tea kettles and headlights, leg made of
human-knee supports, knee made from an upside down coffee pot where a finch
nests. Her gathered branches protrude.

She darts yellow-breasted when I come. A cow's skull for a stallion's
chest, and large pans make the giant stead, hoary-hoofed,
with an exoskeleton of ribs. He's exposed in Minnesota winters.

On hind legs rearing forever a junk-heap, a master of rising—
head as broad as a bull's, he's a testament to waste
and how we can save. Was the fighting pose rage?
The penis erect? Art brut. The horse which no man could mount?

Defense or aggression? We can only guess. Untamed, unruly,
large teeth bite the night. Tail of flyswatters and bent hangers,
mane a garage broom and key chains. Hubcaps for thighs,
a shovel holds his back to a washbasin neck. Material, monstrous
mammal, so like us. Conflict and combat for love? Lust.

Years from now when we are gone, his blue carburetor heart,
metal crutch leg and bed-pan crotch, the baseball bat leg
and bowling shoe haunches will still stand beneath a spring-opened
maw that will howl silence over the prairie.

See beyond his steely gold eye to the bluff's echo. See the eagle
with its five-foot wing span coasting above. We know why the frozen violent
posture appeals to us, how its wreckage springs untamed.

Elegy For Narcissus

He leaned above the nude body,
tight torso of Atlas,
admired his own back curved fetal,
shoulders muscular. Barefoot and naked
before his own image, cheeks blushed and cold,
he whispered, "Forget me not
when I've grown old."

He adored his own cherub face,
dipped his pale forearm into cold green water,
watched it disturb the view.
He mumbled something.

The mouth in the image swallowed
the limb willingly,
in small concentric ripples.
He ignored the large goldfish
that bumped his elbow. The white
ancient one sucked
his thumb. He did not hear
the birds or the rustle of the pines.

Satiated. He removed his hand as
if it were new born. Later,
crouched as an animal, the moon
tugged at the feminine within him.
His thighs lengthy and bare,
muscled in the dark.

Altering as he changed, the body
scorned him. His own watery eyes
held weariness. The evening breeze
broke the surface as if the image said,
I hate you. I have always hated you.

This Is The Way We Come To Light

Inevitably, slowly, the warmth enough to fill
the emptiness. We are forgetting traumas daily.
We're not here to entertain the birds; the trees
do quite well with their own music.

Black spotted leaves strewn along the ground
as she dies. Blackbirds rush
through the air—a symphony of remembrance.

Wild shrieks, hot days billowing through us
like smoke. We are the resurgences of silence,
mystery of days, moon moving through space.

Greedy we are for the moment. Here then gone,
bat wings, sparrows, robins thinly perched
on bare trees, grass quiet with yellow flowers,

the suddenness of spring. She is at once willows
and herons, arroyos and cacti, but today
she turns her back on the distance of planets

for the brief day's light. She is the crackle
of crows, a dog barking repetitively through
the buzz of an electric saw.

Writing The Next Poem

— for *Emmy Pérez*

The universe waits on nothing,
sheds her nebulous hairdo,
her dandruff stars.

We are glorious fools
after nothing again.

I am you, passed
and passing in the empty sky.

"Let go," a friend said,
and I was gone before I knew it,
and you were lost in the music,

the thin high-altitudes of loss,
the high-altitudes of forgotten hunger.

The homeless congregate in big cities;
I keep my change in my pocket,
while here heavy in the grave.

My hand bone fragments
writing a single poem.

Born In The Southwest

I don't know the blue dangers of the city,
or park rangers, and I've never been in a kayak.
No whitewater rapid, no bungee-jump.
I don't know the waves of the ocean or a cruise.

I wish I'd seen him turn water into wine.
And day by day, I sing to the empty air. Once
a white-throated sparrow sang with me
along the arid cares of a vast desert.

I imagine poems of grit and lost snow-capped Sierras,
lost jobs, lost languages, and never have bought
a vacation package. I am lost in the cat's broken
whiskers, the way he is blind in one eye, the torn
cornea of green in a certain slant of light.

I don't know the city coffee shops and thin bodies
rushing to a subway. Everything moving fast.
I am the sand, the horizon long and listless
over the thatched roofs of tar and sweating sky.

A man sleeps all day in a blanket
on the watered grass at the university, and students
wander by afraid. He snores. La Migra on bicycles
nearby with silver-mirrored glasses,

as if they are misplaced insects, or aliens gazing
across brown faces looking for tattered clothes, a
gaze with whiskers that appears broken.

It's like this—
pretend.

Pretend to be something
he's not. Pretend to hold his back straight,
his chest out. All the boldness of a mountain lion
before the shot.

Cabeza De Vaca's Horse

The ear a cavern of bats in New Mexico.
My eyes dark matter. I am Pancho Villa's sombrero.
La Malinche's fire. White water rapids,

I wind like rivers to the sea. Cabeza de Vaca,
conquistador with no desire to raze.
Beneath your fallen horse,

your voice whispered borders, tropical need,
rain dance and prayer. You buried your armor
in the heart of Texas. There is a blaze,

the oldest adobe oven: bread risen, baked, served.
You shared papaya with natives who used you like a mule.
Your feet shreds and blisters, your body sores.

From captive to survivor to friend, nude
in hunger's need you learned to speak slavery's bonds
and thought of a king's appetite.

Spaniards later took you from Buenos Aires to Spain
in chains and shackles. Explorer, warrior, languages
mixed in your bloody mouth.

And borders speak to you like rio and sandstorm.
I imagine you in heaven dressed for summer
in cotton and the breeze a slow undressing.

The sky a lewd embrace. When I open my mouth,
bats emerge as the sunset burns
your long silence.

El Paso Women

Some say *forget*
what birthed a million songs,
split the broken border.

Remember cliffs,
small hidden desert mountain streams,
the work that hands do. The sun's heat
so hot women bake and brew.

Mujer, expect a solar burn,
make a meal of scarcity.

We know prophesy and bruja weeds,
caw magic spells like crows in flight
over blood-spilled Juárez.

The azul river,
an indigo vein,
cerulean birds, rancheras
Indio-lit
with a music that wants

to believe

in a God who suffered, in a land
of milk of honey where olive trees bloom.

       We know a path of tumbleweeds
       and ash, of arroyos and winding hawks.

We see roads as igneous conduits,
a volcanic rush of ash.
Duende and daemon
burn and burst like the tail of a comet,

       and when we see pyramids
       we think only of sacrifice.

Alluvial Heartache

I know but one river, its chain-link fence topped with razor wire,
    torn bits of clothing
        caught and fluttering, border patrol
            jeeps crouched like cats each night.

I have seen its separateness and sorrow.

    Men and women on porches at night listen,
        mariachi music rises, beers lift.
            Children watch stars blink,
later run broken sidewalks.

    Thin-ribbed dogs chained
            close to fences growl.

Cloudy river, sandy rivulet, alluvial heartache.

    Language lost while the satiated third generation
        writes of thirst, leaves with a kiss,
            watching adobe and stucco disappear—

The hawk steals from its own kind.

The sun hot on some backs.

Sleepers and sweepers dark and thin—all things
    overshadow their faces in the end.

Lubbock, Texas 1981

Thorna ran into the street in her underwear.
Solid black muscular quads moved naked
in the breeze. Her ass tightly wound sprinter's
gluteus maximus,
defiant beneath satin
panties.

Her hair pulled back matched the night.
She was careless for fun, words thick
with 13 Amaretto Sours.
She sang a song about law school,
how she was not white.

Neighbors flicked on lights,
and soon the police arrived.

We were young, and Thorna stood firm,
black body sleek, laughing off
wide-eyed dark stares
of those she'd left in the dust.

Thorna was wordy and wild, prickly cactus,
unbroken poem,
sprint across dewy grass.

Such freedom could not be allowed.
The cops arrived.
She was arrested
singing.

La Mano Negra

I let the universe have her way with me,
gendered and purified. We break every rule
archaic and blue, two bodies forgetting
themselves. December, and I dream
daffodils and Texas springtime. New Mexico
moves through mestiza. I hoard pills on
the crowded desk, somewhere between
what really was and dream,
solve equations for 13 months, leave false
friends on their cold doorsteps. I fence well,
fold in on myself like a bat, cormorant
risen from murky water. Slick.
I search out inequalities and keep only primes.
All down the street screen doors slam
as if I carry a gospel of lies.
A woman with a house with no door
swears multitudes have seen my hand,
black as a universe.

❖ ❖ ❖

Gula, glotonería, codicia/ambicíon, avidez
Gluttony, greed, covetousness/ambition, eagerness

"Gluttony is an emotional escape, a sign something is eating us."

— Peter De Vries

"Taste every fruit of every tree in the garden at least once.
It is an insult to creation not to experience it fully.
Temperance is wickedness."

— Stephen Fry

The Healing Poem

She says the gall bladder stores bitterness.
Imagine its stones something of heavy pain:
Burning as if an organ burst.

The way a fireman looks down on a face,
all grimace. She says, "An animal is your totem,
find your guide." Damn the sea gulls' beauty

over the iced parking lot. Squirrels play as maple
leaves fall along damp winter ground. The cold
comes in thick ice, the way a woman breaks

into it with a plastic blade hoping to clear a view.
Blades of grass flower like small white cacti.
There's something askew in the world, the word

gall rings. As if nobody cares for the bitter
escalation of a dark heart. She says, "Never use
the word *dark* or *gall*," but I am dark gall.

My acid deep within. This is my healer; her tale
is of dreaded truths; her hands touch fear;
she seldom cries. She says the gall bladder

stores bitterness. The small incisions cut through,
now the scar beneath my heart red.

Chico's Tacos

A huge roach skitters along your white stucco
outside wall, streets fill with Impalas, Chevys,
cholos, abuelas. Fathers sit at formica tables;
the tile peels. Counter workers speak Spanish.

Women wear polyester and sandals.
Men don letter jackets from years ago.
The lone striped suit and slick expensive shoes,
always some style. The young in tight jeans,

high heels—nothing like a late night dance break
at Chico's where caliente red water *y* dried red chilé-
soaked flautas piled high with cheese, extra cheese,
and indulgence comes like sizzling cola.

The border refinery steams and twin barbed-wire
stretches across the river to protect freedom.
It's really cash, and everyone at Chico's feels it
subliminally in the paper cups.

❀ ❀ ❀

The Indio-beggar, baby hanging off her slanted back,
an old styrofoam cup held out, eyes dusk.
In the past there were droves, Juáreñas, aliens,

now scattered like tumbleweeds across the desert.
The flame at Asarco once ablaze, now snuffed.
Copper smelting killed the land; children can't play
in the sand. Languages mix—

There will be no celebrities, no Lexus,
no thin models, maybe Oscar de la Hoya, mariachis,
the musical song of a city drowning
on the edge of nowhere.

❀ ❀ ❀

You won't find a beach.
Some days sand blows hair hard and skin feels
pecked by a chicken in the valley, near Ysleta,
where the Tigua Indian Casino closed
after East Texas oil men lost their wealth.
Underground water near Hueco Tanks bartered
like people's lives—but you can always find
Chico's tacos being devoured. A small pleasure
for the poor, and those who grow rich return to
Chico's because it's something of home,
something found nowhere else.

And why would anyone care—
it's no blue grass bar, it's no rock-n-roll café—
no, it's slimy, crowded, sweaty. It's full of Mexicans,
a few gringos, *y* viejitas. Great U.S.A., patriotic home,
this is your hidden pleasure domain.

Maquiladora workers in Juárez murdered,
Mexican-Americans hating Mexicans, cumbias,
rancheras, dollar dances, quinciñeras, gay bars,
maricones dance in the streets of Juárez.
Scenic drive overlooks a million lights.

＊ ＊ ＊

There is no full circle back for some.
It's all dry joblessness. Chico's, Lucky's,
and always the wretched university
with its Bhutanese architecture
large and looming on the smoggy border
like some paradoxical crime.

Forty Days

Scrub-brush burning, camel's shade, a brief
respite, albino scorpions, and even cacti stung
in the dunes. God, in an act of mercy, sent manna,
fruit from God, after the ambrosia of goddesses.
Shimmering fruit of our days.

They sank teeth like knives into it, tore
its fleshy skin. Thoughtless and forever hungry,
their cheeks wet with it—sweet sticky
godliness.

Sands fell on the dry sands. For forty years
the manna kept in an omerful, hands like webs
after it. They ate like thieves until they wandered
to Canaan and Rephidim. They ate as animals.

And as always, men and women who are lucky
forget. It is as if they never knew the face
of the desert, forgot there was no water. Moses

thought he'd be stoned. They rebelled for more,
unthankful, forgetting their blessed gifts, saying only,
"I am tired of fruit. I want red-blooded meat."

Carnivorous hearts pumping for it, saying kill,
kill somebody; kill something, for God's sake.

Elegy for a Warrior

— If you stop chasing the butterfly, it will land on your shoulder.

— Sharon Niles

Friend, gone to the frolicking speed of light?
Gone through my soul. Shot through, a comet.
Your fiery will launched across earth.

I see myself: Water-bearer,
born of dust in the desert.

You inferno, ram-like, fire sign
still triggering sparks.

We are with trees beneath bluffs
seeking solitude. I'm seeking you
in clouds and a crow cawing seven times.

Brown-eyed Cajun woman, you
taught animal totems, believed
in Indian spirit guides.

When stars come you arrive again cosmic—
piqued, and I imagine wild love-making
beneath a Picasso diamond blue-white sky.

You said to visit the pavilion
where hundreds of butterflies
would land on me. Every color borne
on my shoulder as I stand still and wait.

You knew how to live one life
like Warhol and Chagall,
sing like George Harrison
on a bad hair day, belt out operatic.
Star-fire: You were all swing and sway,
all Louisiana bayou.

I'm going home,
where the Rockies loom,
split from the ages, raised
from Earth's turmoil.

I will hike to the top of Lion Gulch
and watch horses trot up the steep trail,
gaze on elk grazing below.

I'm headed to Yellowstone,
where the dead will meet me
again in the ever-changing clouds.

Codicia, ambicíon, avidez/benevolencia, caridad

Greed, ambition, eagerness or covetousness/benevolence, charity

"For greed all nature is too little."

— Lucius Amaeus

"I do not give lectures or a little charity. When I give I give myself."

— Walt Whitman

The Damselfly

A singer's high-pitched sorrow fled the world.
Blind in flight, twelve dragonflies rose
black as bees to the sound of it.

Heads so human it was odd,
hovering over the prairie
as if they knew they were alive.

You on the riverbed, I imagine alive
while damselflies alight on the tops of reeds
feet clinging to curved stems above
a spider's web.

Twelve damselflies teaching stillness.

On the prairie, dragonflies, four-winged,
no damsels, rush mad for light.
Ravenous, they charge hundreds of fireflies.

Hunger leads them as night falls over pink flowers.
Still, the damselflies sit as wind blows the reeds,
teaching us to wait for beauty.
And you, dear friend, were such contentedness.

I follow Swainson's hawk soaring over
the wildly buzzing prairie. I am seeking a sign
as my feet sink into mud. There are trees
leaning to worship the sun, speaking stillness.

Red with bites, seeking myself,
seeking you, demanding the dead
present themselves
and their story.

Stars Emerge From Every Conceivable Place

You once gathered storms and let loose
a procession of drums. Beaten child,
unruly Cajun, you're pandemonium.

Your deep voiced songs hurl
shooting stars, a white Niagara falling.
You named me change-agent, said chaos

was my destiny, told me we'd lived together
a thousand lifetimes. And what are eons
when we are alive, stirring disarray?

I dug myself a rut in the desert of my birth.
You spoke yin and yang,
chimed a tune about the cosmos.

You healed all wounds except your own.
I dream loons and dragons, a window opening,
dream of your return.

Maybe you found the pulse you sought, and you're finally
all vibration and space, guiding lost spirits.
Wild hippy of Mexico, you spoke planes of existence

as my eyes rolled. Sky swept you back to ash, and I forgot
stars, the lone cypress deep in the Mississippi.
The sea inside eclipsed the entire sky.

The Loser

Although I lost the car, the house, the better job,
my eyes wander everywhere and nowhere.

I'll dive deep into the water, splash
my animal hair. My torso sunned
and bare. I'll grow strawberries and melons,

and my vegetables will bloom dark green.
I'll dream and un-dream a million old things,
own a gazebo, a stone bridge, a palomino.

My imaginary cottage will have birdsong
and shade. The sun will purchase my gaze.
I'll count heaven in my forgotten language.

Weary of salesmen who want me to sell time,
I wander lush-lazy to and fro, sing
while trees are taken by light.

Hustlers wear their shoes shined. I am barefoot
in the stream. They left us behind
among daffodils floating in the light.
Crab-apple blossoms ebb white with sky.

Not One Red Cent

I steal toilet paper,
boil beans and garlic,
bless and baptize pennies.

Kabala: forbearance
in face of insult.

America, I am a connoisseur
of the divided dollar.

For some, a sticky nickel found
comes as joyous as love.

E Pluribus Unum sounds dirty.
Graven image beneath a dirty thumb,

each of my cents declares
someone else's trust in God.

Some say, *God is everywhere*—
even in a copper smelter's lungs.

I count them out on the counter
while the clerk rolls blue eyes,
sets her hand on a fat hip.

She sighs, moves them two by two
into the arc of her palm.

I want to write about whales,
think of Jonah in the belly of one,
punished then expunged onto land.

I walk unlike Jonah,
wool cap pulled over my ears thinking,
I am not welcome anywhere.

For The Fire Happy Boss And Owner At 7-11
On Ralston And Wadsworth In What Surely
Is The Middle Of Hell: Arvada, Colorado

You have fired everyone and rehired some twice.
Yesterday you worked graveyard, and I received
the dreaded call. "Come back! Please!!!"

I wanted to say: May you gorge on red coconut Twinkies,
Zingers, Honey Buns, Hot Tamales, Snickers, Paydays, Hot-Pockets
and processed foods. But I said, "I'll come in."

The wages of sin are death. "Thank heaven for 7-11" is a decoy
phrase meant to distract. Yes, you sell cheap beer, tobacco
and lotto tickets, male enhancement products,
energy drinks and chew.

Every addiction purchased with hijacked over-run prices:
Kodiak, Copenhagen, Skoal long cut, pouches.
Every brand of smokes: Kools, Marlboro.
Every brand of watered down beer. Oh queen

of junk food and beef jerky, may you be condemned

to forever drink Lone-Star Beer
and eat fake licorice.

May you void and void every transaction and hand
each dollar out to homeless vagabonds everywhere.

May you be forced to take the bus daily with sacks
of over- priced milk. May you fear being fired daily
from your minimum wage doppelganger.

It's not easy; you're tutoring among the grime;
toothbrush in hand, I'm detail cleaning towards death.

May you lay off all cursed employees
so they can collect unemployment benefits.

May you lose every lotto you enter: Scratch Game,
Powerball, Cash Five, Mega-Millions, State Lotto.

May your diet consist of stale over-bleached white
bread and rancid peanut butter.

It was not easy watching you and your false sympathy
for the poor. But you're not evil,
just a little greedy for winter.

Every Loser Surprises The World

The homeless woman dressed dark in sunshine
caresses a wrinkled envelope with coins.
In heavy boots and a leaf-covered coat,
she curses God and blesses cigarettes.

Her grocery cart overflows with blankets,
but I turn and give nothing.
I am holding onto my own.

Cold before winter's white, a man paints
beauty with slick oils, wood easel in yellow grass.

Blessed be the poor in heart,
crimson vines falling over rock
framing each autumn. Two homeless men curse
the Mexicans, then chuckle behind dirty beards.

Panhandlers a menace today,
with disappointed frowns they ask, "Spare change?"
I shut them down. My eyes steely in morning dew.
I walk to work where the boss keeps secrets
in hidden closets.

Maybe, the trees will save us. The rush
of the rising Platte filled with plastic bottles;
ducks madly beat the air. Wings work

overtime, necks stretch forward. Each spring
they pair off with their lovers. In June, ducklings
stream grassy enclaves along the bank.

A pair of jeans soaked, trapped by a log, half buried
in black water. A young man murdered and found
without his pants.

Mortar

My father used to grind cement and water, pour a misshapen
   surface, always in a hurry. "You're not sorry," he would mock.

The desert full of broken adobe homes, fences unpainted, rot.
   The canal slithers in crawdads and mosquitoes, a boy carries
the last bull-frog before the rush of pesticide. I dreamed of jackals
   running through the streets of El Paso. Father drove us to sugarcane
fields, and we tasted the sweet hard cane. He said, "Anything sweet
   comes in hard sweat," and the sun glared on our dark heads.

God always said, "I will pour out water on the thirsty land."
   His spirit poured like cement, like lava into stone monuments
of murderous Spaniards. Amá took us to the Wonder Bread Bakery.
   She said, "It is important not to burn the bread." The kingdom
of God is leaven. It takes a fire.

Pompeii, frozen men at work forever, how it came suddenly,
   the way kingpins bury men in cement, how God said,
"Be dried up!" This desert all mud-homes, all rock fences.
   Muzzle-loaded cannons fired. Always rushed, my father joined
bricks and stones in drunkenness. I am crushed with a pestle.

   God's thunderous warnings half-remembered again and again
while I imagine bricklayers with straightedges
   spreading depth to a perfect form. Hurried and frazzled,
there is no time for a smooth calculated foundation.

Heat wavers over a city along the Mexican border,
 sizzling bronze statues of conquistadors. High fences,
razor-wire and guards gaze, while weary bricklayers forget.

 They work in silence, their breath hot air, their hands
careful, and it is as if brujas stirred a scarecrow
 of mud and straw, and men far away write of sackcloth
and ash and often fire leaves only ash.

There is no breath in the statue of a dead Spaniard. Molten
 eyes gaze vacantly over the city. He sits on a stallion
of plaster before a museum of half-truths. He sits like a forced song
 in the ear, like a jewel before hungry mouths.

Ouray's Eyes

—Photo: Chief Ouray of the Ute tribe of Colorado
Born in Taos in 1833, dead at 47 after a trip to D.C.

Your eyes held the gray in the world
with dead-eyed dignity.

Hands thick, lips turned downward
in a small frown. You knew four languages,
wore a vest with a timepiece
in the left pocket; they called you

savage: Ute, Apache,
Spanish, English. No smile,
only a subtle turn away
from the camera. They called you

diplomat, friend of whites. Feigning
friendship to keep your people alive.
In your gray eyes, subdued rage,
an arrow shot.

Braves hold our gaze, ask
the same old questions of genocide.

And what of the silence?

We profess our innocence,
yet none of us clean
enough to gaze back.

Envidia/benevolencia, amabilidad

Envy/benevolence, kindness

"Envy is the ulcer of the soul."

— Socrates

"Be humble, for the worst thing in the world is of the same stuff as you; be confident, for the stars are made of the same stuff as you."

— Nicholai Velimirovic

The Wounded Healer

There is a city inside my eye,
a stone bridge where the oldest healers
sit, then unfold like blue herons.

My teacher, surely you knew Chiron's rejection,
how his mother fled his image early with disgust.
Child born of a rape, the initial wounding—
Who would trade immortality for the gift of fire?
The psychic wound and the physical scar,
a parent's deception and disinterest.

You, mentor, were everything at once yet singular.
Your hands were sea and fire.
You said to me, "You must see your hidden gifts."

Healer, physician, mender of wounds, circling
in erratic highly eccentric orbit. Elliptical,
some say you are traversing between Saturn
and Uranus in a fifty-year trek,
to complete the cycle around the sun.

My master musician, healer, my friend,
you escape the Kuiper belt with Chiron,
orbit beyond Pluto in myth.

Centaur star, comet-lit, friend to flame,
I am finally learning to lose the shame.

Coming Home

— after Sherwin Bitsui

No chance to be wedded,
biblically or not,
when one is born to the border
and its crossings. Men suffocating
in trucks, women weighted with children.

Georgia, I imagine green and lush,
Alabama, ivy and willows, sunlight's jagged
leaves, Louisiana, streams of grass and waters
ebb to the oily Gulf.

Destiny rafts the muddy rivers of our lives.
Langston Hughes sang of his muddy river
and misplacement.

I am displaced metaphor, a misunderstood
import for desert people brown and happy
as windy sand pecks El Paso's dove-eyed faces.

I always wanted more than weeds,
tumbleweeds, miles of loose sand
rushing air and sandy hills.

I misused myself in want, ran to the west
and found rivers bubbling with white rush.
The lakes murky, and naked swimmers dive
deep into foam and shiver.

The desert is a place without want.
It is the plastic bags of shoppers on smoky buses,

a shadowy man running across
the highway. Running as if he were unreal, as if
he were no longer human.

So, I return with stickers in my socks, the mean cry.
Today, I am weary of poetry, weary of this mist,
this conglomerate of happy criticism.

I return to the crude language of my ancestors,
to the beauty of loss, so sullen in the blue sky
which always rises after the clearing
and the settling of want.

Sisters

I lost her friendship the summer it cost me two others.
I was loyal Aquarius, loyal as a lover, loyal as a sister.
Attraction comes and goes like leaves in seasons.
The artists walk with lunch pails towards creation.

The morning steamy and foggy, the trees arching.
She was my obsession and envy, full of need
she turned away, turned toward something:
herself.
I was an unanswered prayer towards un-loneliness.

I loved the drama of rejection. She was
spaces and silences. I was myself and myself,
a surreal hunger. I was dreaming Van Gogh,
dreaming Degas' dancers.
I was barefoot in the painting of my life.

She was disastrous divorces, the bang-up hang-up.
I was loud colors, the pitch of trombones and trumpets.
She was flutes, at the most, a high-strung piccolo.
I'd found my man; she'd lost hers.

I was the endless eye of hunger. She was depleted giving.
It was time to let go, let go like the opening up of a poem.
I'm wishing her a poem, envy gone,
the letters unwritten and unheard.

Dawn

Language has hid its huge lids, its dark pupils
in the aftermath of my trauma. Too brutal to tell,
I am remembrance after decades of forgetting.

The best story is outside the *self*. Impermanence,
breath and sight. April snow comes expected,
yet still a surprise after apple-blossoms bloom.

To be spontaneous song, cling to the emptiness.
We are intertwined yet alone, at times mindless
cattle, a herded perseverance.

But today, I will sit in silence: the scene full white,
even the bare branches lit with it, and the light
comes soon enough. We are the now, the habitual

patterns of grasping and fixation, the sights
and sounds, a flotsam of reflections. Cherry-
blossoms survive winter's last gasp,

not unlike looking through trauma clear-eyed,
finding rapture in another's eyes, the irises
healing. Meditation's silence; we help one another

and the sea inside subsides. He said, after the cancer,
"We are all divine." The wind comes the next day
and the light snow melts, and the grass begins greening.

The world a dark blue glistening, and we,
the brief light, the spectacular gods, the whirling
disbelief we are but shadow and shine.

Survivors

We come to abuse through memory, sudden flash, assault.
The way a young body flails and falls, the forgetting

a blessing. But at forty-seven the cost of memory
too high? What's begging your pardon for

when all you do is say you're sorry for everything,
for the other person's rising rages,

for your very presence? Wounded
out of the blocks, they say, one can heal. Loss

is wintry steel or refinery smoke, years passing
like tumbleweeds—Yet, we are as thorny-crowned

gods, as talented thieves, as evening's almost full moon,
drawing our liquid bodies. We are more than

cells dividing and space. And here,
a watery mirror, the lake filling with geese.

Today, lilacs and lavender, cars line the park,
cherry blossoms and the first tulip orange and open.

Meditative blessings, breath and heartbeat,
and we are as reunion and movement. We do not speak

of it, but like bodies in crowds, bodies
in the open field, we are detailed glimmers.

Appearances and masks lost in remembrance, a keen
seeing. We are great actors when forgetting,

Lethe leading us to doubt ourselves.
Trauma, unspeakable, a conviction

leans towards healing, and we are slowly whole, content
with the mirror, content with the sway of our own hips.

Small Defiant Gods

I weep for none and shed my hair like aspen leaves.
I wander aimlessly alone, come sullen and sacred
at the end of winter. I bow to no one

and send no love. What needs of yours or mine
are known? I whisper no language, require no wit.
If you find me, I will tell you no poem.

I quake not, nor remember. Flirtatious
and haughty, I offer no visions, bother not
with prophecy or prayer. I have no voice, no song.

I come to you no lover, no fool and never reminisce;
my breath is cool, then hot. I move darkness,
then light, hold the sun like a toy, the stars like dust.

I know no marriage, no birth or death.
Slow soundlessness follows me, and I offer you
no image, no bone or sex. Some call me Dark Mother.

If you find me at the precipice of your cold heart,
I may simply shrug. Some say spirits haunt you
and the un-favored dead hang on, but you really doubt

anything beyond my darkest eye. I smile
for no one; my black skirt trails everything.
Faceless I taunt; you pretend. I move;

corpses spread over the surface of the earth
like stones. Some say the end of my journey is God,
some say the journey itself is creation, but you know

the hands that hold you are bone and ash, so what moves you
through me like small defiant gods? Your brief living,

breath and word hurl beyond my notice, and I bind you,
in hunger like blind prophets singing before I come to reap.
My womb is starry, my number is nine.

Radiance

The stars blink a wondrous explosion;
expansion loosens, a crane in flight.

I saw a man's hands calloused and yellowed
with smoke. He swore the world was cold,
he'd speak his dirty mind,

and how he'd glide, lottery ticket in hand,
motion-filled and greedy for change,
but he'd sit all day and smoke,
emphysema be damned.

My step-father died afraid, full of regret.

His body shook and jerked as mine once did.
Forgiveness is darkly lit. I saw him in red
clouds, imagined him in his own hell.

You and I and he careen
'round corners of black space,
and distance is seemingly lost in breath,
touch, and madness. We are but images

and sound, tactile hope, and we lean
towards one another protectively grieving
losses. Islands and oceans, ink-haired
or blonde as a sun, we isolate, abuse,
draw towards one another.

We are moving through the days' sinew
and rant, voyeurs to magic. Our steps
light then heavy, the seasons within
a rebirth. Hurtling through this stark
universe, we are light and radiance.

Our wants lost in solitude
and prayer, we are taught best
on the streets where light
pursues our brief blossoming.

Recovery

We were voiceless children, offered up
for the entitlement of others. We were as mimes,
our faces hidden beneath make-up.

Our hands, the hands of children,
our bodies shocked into adulthood.

When I was a child I prayed to God,
turned to what's visible—
saints glistening in blue windows,
a priest gathering sins up into the coals.

My father, a figure in the corner,
a sharp headless looming, a disastrous need
I could not name sin.
Easier to forget, and forget I did.

Praise the child of Lethe,
and this woman now remembers violence.

I want to believe in something miraculous,
but the sea of sky calls me to sobriety.
God wasn't a figure or a form. God, a summer respite

after the breaking. You can beg for forgiveness,
but we must first forgive our limitations.
We rise with the pink sunrise, the crazy coos of birds,

the silence of waking. We are children,
blooms and flickering stars.
As a child, the desert sun set wildly red.

We are the first heron on the stillest lake,
ribbons of moonlight cast along water.

About The Author

Sheryl Luna earned a PhD in contemporary literature from the University of North Texas and an MFA from University of Texas, El Paso. Her first collection, *Pity the Drowned Horses*, received the Andres Montoya Poetry Prize and was published by the University of Notre Dame Press. It was a finalist for the National Poetry Series and the Colorado Book Award.

Luna was awarded fellowships from the Corporation of Yaddo, the Anderson Center, the Ragdale Foundation and CantoMundo. She received the Alfredo Cisneros del Moral Foundation Award from Sandra Cisneros in 2008. She has taught at the University of Colorado at Boulder and Metropolitan State College of Denver.

About The Artist

Brooke Shaden was born in March of 1987 in Lancaster, Pennsylvania and grew up near the Amish Country. Brooke was photographically born in December of 2008 after graduating from Temple University where she received degrees in film and English.

She began creating self-portraits for ease and to have full control over the images. Self-portraiture for her is not autobiographical in nature. Instead, Brooke attempts to place herself within worlds she wishes we could live in, where secrets float out in the open, where the impossible becomes possible.

Brooke works to create new worlds within her photographic frame. By using painterly techniques as well as the square format, traditional photographic properties are replaced by otherworldly elements. Brooke's photography questions the definition of what it means to be alive.